REAL TENN[

For

REAL TENNIS
PLAYERS

SIMPLE TIPS TO HELP YOU
PLAY BETTER TENNIS FAST

by
Kim Selzman

Real Tennis Tips for Real Tennis Players:
Simple Tips to Help You Play Better Tennis Fast

© 2014 by Kim Selzman
All Rights Reserved.

Table of Contents

INTRODUCTION

"Start where you are. Use what you have. Do what you can. "

- **Arthur Ashe,** *former World No. 1 and winner of 3 Grand Slam singles titles*

It's easy to get caught up in the belief that your tennis play will improve if you just spend more time or more money on the sport. If you just get a better racquet. Or better shoes. Or spend hours and hours on court in private lessons. Or watching instructional DVDs. Or attending another drill, clinic, or boot camp. And while some of those things might help, maybe, you can also get better without them.

That's where this book comes in. *Real Tennis Tips for Real Tennis Players* was written for players like you and like me - "real" tennis players. Average, everyday players who want to get better fast. We're not

professional athletes. We may not be in the best physical shape. We're short on time and we don't want to waste our money. And, unfortunately, we're often frustrated with our lack of improvement. We want to play better tennis and we want to do it now!

The good news is that we *can* get better at tennis and we can do it quickly. We can do it by learning and applying some simple tips. "Real" tennis tips that can really work for "real" tennis players.

That's what you'll find in this book - tips that will work for you. These tips aren't secrets that no one has ever revealed before. They're just basic tips that can quickly amp up your game but that a lot of players either forget about or are completely oblivious to.

How do I know this? Because the first time I finally got a "real" tennis tip, my own game dramatically changed for the better.

I was in my weekly private lesson, for which I paid $70 an hour. Like many recreational players, I had been taking private lessons for months and months but hadn't seen any incredible change in my game. I don't even like to think about how much money I'd put into those lessons. Anyway, I was practicing my serve at the end of my lesson, just as I'd always done.

 5

But this time, as I was preparing to hit yet another weak, ineffective serve, my coach said something to me that he'd never said before: "Be sure and target your serve."

Target my serve? I'd never even thought about targeting my serve. Like a lot of players, I was just hitting my serve and hoping it landed somewhere, anywhere, in the service box.

But something about that one little tip - target your serve - changed everything. Instead of my serve being something that was unreliable at best and embarrassing at worst, targeting my serve transformed it into a reliable, useful part of my game. Something that I could use to control what would happen in points. Something that I could actually, on occasion, call a weapon.

With that one tennis tip, it was as if a light bulb went off in my head. If that tip could do so much for me, what could a whole slew of great tips do?

After that, I became a "hoarder" of tennis tips. I wrote them down in notes I kept in my tennis bag. I kept lists of them on my bulletin board at home. I discussed them with members of my tennis teams. I badgered my tennis coach for more of them. I began

a website, *TennisFixation.com*, and blogged about them. I even started a podcast just to talk about tennis tips - the *Tennis Quick Tips* podcast on iTunes.

But, most importantly, I tried them out. In my matches and in my practices, I applied any tennis tip that I thought might make some difference in the quality of my game, no matter how small.

Some worked great - the obvious tip to carry plenty of water and snacks to every match has proved invaluable in several three setters. Some weren't so helpful - hit my forehand as if I'm hitting "through a loaf of bread"? I'm still trying to figure that one out.

Over time, I was able to cull down my collection of tennis tips into the best ones, the ones that really work. And that's what you'll find in this book - real tennis tips that work for real tennis players.

In this book, I give you all of the great tennis tips that I've discovered that I believe will quickly and easily improve your game - tips that you can put into action right away to see real results.

You may already know some of these tips. Others will be brand new. My recommendation is that you quickly read through the entire book and then return to those chapters that you are most excited about. For example, if want to improve your serve, focus on *Chapter III. The Serve & The Return*. Try out those tips out that seem most eye-opening to you. Highlight those tips, pack this book in your tennis bag, go over the tips before your next match, and then apply them to your game. When you've adopted the ones that work for you, try out the tips in other chapters. Keep applying tips as your game progresses.

The truth is the best tennis player is not necessarily the one who practices the most, or has the most powerful serve or knows the best strategies to use in every situation. Rather, tennis is a game that often rewards the player who does just a few things, sometimes only one thing, better than his or her opponent. Just a few minor adjustments can make all the difference between playing fun, easy-going, enjoyable tennis and tennis that makes you want to throw your racquet over the fence and call it a day.

I hope that *Real Tennis Tips for Real Tennis Players* will give you many, many tips for making those minor adjustments that pay off big. Ultimately, I hope this book will help you become the kind of tennis player you've always wanted to be.

EQUIPMENT,
GEAR & ACCESSORIES

"Most players figure they're ready for the match if they bring along tennis shoes, socks, shorts, shirt, racket, and a jockstrap or sports bra. They're all set right there - they're hoping the opponent will bring the tennis balls. A player who's serious about winning goes beyond the bare minimum . . . ."

- Brad Gilbert, *former Top 10 tennis player, well-known coach and commentator, in his book* <u>*Winning Ugly*</u>

If you want to win in tennis, having the right equipment, gear and accessories on court is of paramount importance. Not only do you need the best gear for your game, but you need the extra accessories that help you play your best.

1. **Use the best tennis racquet for your game.** The most important piece of tennis equipment you take out onto the court with you `is your tennis racquet. Spend the time and the money to get the racquet that works best for your game. You can find plenty of up-to-date information about tennis racquets by reading on-line guides and by talking to the pros in tennis specialty stores.

2. **Always pack at least two racquets in your tennis bag.** No matter what level of player you are, even if you're an absolute beginner, you should always carry at least two tennis racquets with you. At some point, you will break a string and having that second racquet saves you from having to forfeit your match. You may also find that one of your racquets just "feels" better on some days, probably because of the tension of the strings. You'll also make it much easier on yourself when you need to have a racquet restrung as you can always play with your second racquet.

3. **Have your racquet strung properly.** Having the right strings on your racquet at the right tension is incredibly important because those strings are the only thing that should be coming into contact with the tennis ball. Consult with your stringer about the proper tension and type of string you should use that will work best for your racquet and your style of play.

4. **Restring your racquet when necessary.** The rule of thumb is you should restring your racquet as many times per year as you play per week. So, if you play about three times a week, you should restring about three times per year. You can also take a look at your strings and see just how worn and fuzzy they're getting. If they look like they're about to break, it's time to restring.

5. **Take care of your racquet.** Temperature can affect both your racquet and your strings. So take care to store your racquets, and your other tennis equipment, properly. Do not leave your racquets, or your tennis bag, in your car overnight where temperatures can really fluctuate and have an impact on your equipment.

6. **Use a non-stick product to prevent your racquet from slipping.** There are a number of products that you can apply to the handle of your racquet or to your hands to prevent your racquet from slipping on contact with the ball. A grip overwrap is a fabric wrap that you put over the grip of your racquet that can absorb moisture and add extra cushioning. You can also try rosin or various sticky gels or balms that you apply directly to your hands. Whatever product you choose, be sure and keep extra supplies in your tennis bag so that your racquet always feels comfortable during match play.

7. **Replace your tennis shoes when necessary.** Your tennis shoes give you support, cushioning and traction on the court so wearing good shoes is important. Check if it's time for a new pair by looking at the bottom of your shoe. The "outsole" of the shoe is the bottom covering that contacts the court. It should be patterned with waves or grooves to provide traction. If the outsole is starting to wear away so that you can see the layers underneath and the traction is losing depth, it's time to get a new pair of shoes. Another rule of thumb - if you play 2 to 3 times a week, you probably need a new pair of shoes 2 to 3 times a year.

8. **Know *The Rules of Tennis*, *The Code*, and the rules for your league and keep a copy of these items in your tennis bag.** Eventually, you are going to get into some kind of rules conflict during a match and the person who knows the rule, or at least seems to know the rule, is usually the one who wins the point. So, read through *The Rules* and *The*

Code periodically to refresh your knowledge. And be aware of any special rules that might apply in your league matches. Do not lose or give away points because you do not know the rules.

9. **Always pack a can of new tennis balls in your bag.** Do not add to your own stress by forgetting to bring new tennis balls to your match. Even if you are not required to provide balls, this ensures that you will always play your matches with new, bouncy balls, hopefully ones that are appropriate for your court. A can of used balls in your bag is great to use for practice.

10. **Use the right balls for your tennis court.** Tennis balls come with two types of felt coverings – regular-duty and extra-duty. Regular-duty or "soft court" balls are designed for use on clay courts and have a thinner, less fuzzy felt covering so that the balls will pick up less clay when used on those courts. Extra-duty or "hard court" balls are for use on hard and grass courts. Their felt covering is thicker and they have more fuzz on them, allowing them to be used longer on hard courts. If you play on clay a lot, regular-duty balls will perform better and last a little longer. If you play on hard courts or grass a lot, extra-duty balls will not only have a longer life, but that extra fuzz may help a bit with increasing the spin you can put on the ball.

11. **For quick energy, eat something.** If you're hungry, your energy is low and you're definitely not going to play your best tennis. You'll also be prone to muscle fatigue and cramps. Be sure to eat a healthy meal well in advance of your match and pack a portable snack to munch on between sets. Good options include granola bars, nuts, and bananas.

12. **Always stay hydrated.** Failing to properly hydrate before and during your match can leave you physically and mentally exhausted. Extreme dehydration can result in cramping, heat exhaustion, and even heat stroke. It's critical to drink up before you hit the court and to sip often while you're playing, on every changeover at least. The best on-court drink is also the cheapest - water. Because other players, teams and clubs may have different ideas about how much water you need to play or how you can best get access to it, always bring your own water with you.

13. **Bring a towel to your match.** A towel is a necessity on court. It's great for wiping off sweat or stopping a nose bleed. It's great for wiping down your racquet. You can pour some water on it and use it to cool off. You can hide under it if you need some alone time to contemplate your strategy.

14. Apply sunscreen before your match starts.
While you know you should always wear sunscreen when playing tennis, do not wait to apply it until the middle of your match. Not only does this reduce its effectiveness, but thinking about whether or not you should have already applied sunscreen can detract from your focus on court. Pack a spray sunscreen to allow for quick and clean application on changeovers.

15. Carry bandages, pain medications, safety pins and other first aid items in your tennis bag.
Always keep typical first aid, emergency-type items in your tennis bag. You can be sure that every few matches, you will need one of these items or someone on your court will.

16. Carry all necessary phone numbers in your tennis bag.
Do not ever be in the position of forfeiting a match because you show up at the wrong court or you don't know where your partner is. Keep the phone numbers of your team captains, your

teammates, and your regular playing partners in your tennis bag to avoid these situations.

17. **Keep a pen and paper in your tennis bag.** These items are great for keeping score, writing yourself notes, and jotting down lessons or tips you pick up during tennis play. Try to write at least one note to yourself about every match you play and you will soon have a great collection of personal tennis tips.

18. **Make sure your tennis bag is packed with** *your essentials.* Keep your bag loaded with anything and everything you might need to feel comfortable and ensure your best play. If changing into a dry shirt or clean socks midway through a match makes you feel better, be sure and pack those items in your bag.

MATCH PREPARATION
& THE WARM-UP

"Spectacular performances are preceded by spectacular preparation."

- Frank Giampaolo, *top tennis coach and author of The Tennis Parents' Bible*

If you want to get a jump start on your match and your opponents, be sure you begin your preparation well before you arrive on court and that you make the most of your on-court warm-up.

1. Begin the mental warm-up for your match early. Start focusing on your match well before you arrive on court. Visualize what you hope to accomplish. Look over any notes and remind yourself how you want to play your match.

2. **Begin your physical warm-up before you step on court.** Take the time to do some pre-match stretching and cardio exercises that will get your body loose and limber and will get your heart pumping. Examples of tennis-specific moves that you can perform before your match that require no equipment include dynamic stretches, jogging in place, jumping jacks, lunges, and squats.

3. **Size up your opponent.** Pay attention to your opponent as soon as you step on court with him or her. Notice his or her tendencies during the warm-up. By the time the match gets going, you should know several things about your opponent and what his or her strengths and weaknesses are. Does he avoid his backhand? Does she hit weak volleys? Is he slow to get to balls? Does she have a weak serve? You can use all of this information to develop your initial strategy for playing your opponent and gaining an extra edge over him or her before the match even starts.

4. **Immediately determine if your opponent is a righty or a lefty.** Surprisingly, many players don't do this. But it is important to note right from the beginning as it will determine a lot about where you serve and the target of many of your shots.

5. **Determine the physical condition of your opponent.** Is your opponent young or old? Is he on the heavy side or is he pretty fit? Does she move quickly or slowly? Will he tire out easily? You'll play people differently depending on how they appear to be moving. If you play an older, heavy-set opponent, you'll most likely run him or her around and try to tire him or her out. With a younger, fitter player, you may have to be more consistent, more accurate in your shot placement, and you may have to try to make him or her hit clean winners to beat you.

6. **Determine the mental attitude of your opponent.** Watch for any mental tendencies or weaknesses your opponent may show during the warm-up. Some players will easily reveal a lot to you about their mental state - they'll tell you how distracted they are. They'll tell you how the weather conditions bother them. They'll be very chatty and friendly, showing they expect the same of you. Or they'll be very cold and business-like, showing how much they hate chattiness and friendliness. Pay attention to these little mental tells during the warm-up and try to take advantage of them during your match.

7. **In doubles, decide which of your opponents is the weak link.** The most basic strategy in doubles is to pick on the weaker player. During the warm-up, you need to pay attention as to who that might be. This means you need to pay attention to both of your opponents - the one you are warming up with as well as the one your partner is warming up with. Be sure to look over and see what that other opponent looks like and what he or she is doing. During the warm-up, before the match starts, be sure and talk to your own partner about what you picked up on during the warm-up as well as what he or she saw. While some of these observations may be about one of the partner's weaker shots or serving tendencies, they should also be about who appears to be weaker, who is less consistent, who is the team leader, and what kind of personalities are involved.

8. **Be prepared for cold weather tennis.** You'll find that, when temperatures dip, balls are not as bouncy, your racquet strings are less springy, and your body moves more slowly. So be ready to hit harder and deeper than you're used to and try coming into the net a lot. This will help compensate for the changes that cold weather brings to your game.

9. **Be prepared for warm weather tennis.** In warm weather, balls will bounce higher, your racquet strings are looser and springier, and you can become dehydrated quickly. Keep your strokes under control, drink plenty of fluids, and reapply sunscreen often.

THE SERVE & THE RETURN

"You live and die by the serve."

- Pete Sampras, *former World No. 1, and winner of 14 Grand Slam singles titles*

With just a bit of effort, in a short amount of time, and without costly lessons, you *can* significantly improve your serve. By applying just a few of the tips given in this section, your serve can become more powerful, more accurate, and a tool that you can use to gain control of points.

1. **Use the Continental grip.** The best grip for the vast majority of serves and servers is the Continental grip. Obtain this grip by holding your racquet like you would hold a hammer (not like you would hold a frying pan). While it may feel awkward at first, this is the best grip for getting pronation, speed and spin on your serve.

2. **Use a service ritual to relax and focus.** Before every serve, go through the same motions to calm yourself, release any tension in your body, and focus on your next serve. If you don't have a ritual, here's a simple one to try - take your service stance at the baseline, bounce the ball three times, decide what your serve target is, inhale deeply, and then hit your serve.

3. **Use a relaxed and fluid service motion.** The best way to add more power to your serve is to use a loose and relaxed service motion. If you try to "muscle" the ball, your arm will often be locked and stiff, actually resulting in a decrease in power because you're unable to accelerate your racquet through the motion. You can adopt this type of motion by initially concentrating on a slower, more fluid motion. As your swing becomes more comfortable and relaxed, you can accelerate to increase your racquet head speed.

4. **Develop a good ball toss.** Because the ball toss is the motion that actually gets your serve going, it is the most important part of your serve. A good toss places the ball at exactly the right spot for you to hit it. The toss sets off the timing for your entire service motion. If your toss is done properly and consistently, all of the moving parts of your serve will all come together at exactly the right space and time to give you a fighting chance at having a good serve. It is therefore worth spending the time to practice and develop a good ball toss.

5. **Know what a good toss is *not*.** A good toss is not a throw. A good toss does not have a lot of spin on it. A good toss does not travel in a curving path.

6. **Only hit a good toss.** Since you can toss the ball as many times as you want on your serve, you should only hit a good toss - one that travels straight and slightly into the court. Do not be lazy and hit a bad toss just to get the point going.

7. **Hold the ball on its sides, in your fingers.** Hold the ball on the sides with your fingers to ensure a smoother toss. Do not hold the ball in the palm on your hand as the result will be more of a throw than the gentle tossing motion you're looking for.

8. **Picture a good toss.** A great way to imagine what a good toss looks like is to picture the tennis ball as a glass of water. You hold this glass of water firmly but gently. Then you toss the glass of water into the air without spilling a single drop.

9. **Toss in a straight, determinable line.** While the exact placement of your toss may change depending on where you're trying to target your serve or what kind of serve you're hitting, a good ball toss is one that goes up smoothly, in a straight, determinable line.

10. **Toss the ball into the court.** Your toss doesn't necessarily travel in a straight line up into the air, perpendicular to the baseline. It should actually travel in a straight line that angles into the court, especially on your first serve. This is because, by the time your racquet makes contact with the ball, your racquet will have moved forward, slightly in front of you, and into the court.

11. **Toss your ball to the highest distance you can reach.** Your toss should not be too high or too low. If your service motion has a long pause in it, then your toss is probably too high. If your service motion feels rushed, then your toss may be too low. Adjust the height of your toss so that your motion is a continuous, fluid motion resulting in your hitting arm being completely extended and fully reaching up for the ball as contact is made.

12. **Practice your toss with the "toss your socks" drill.** You can perfect your toss by practicing. The "toss your socks" drill can be done inside or outside, on or off the court, at any time. To do it, take a pair of socks, wad them up into a roll, and practice tossing them up using the glass of water visual. If you're a righty, start with the sock roll in your left hand, holding it with your fingers to the sides. Your weight should be shifted into your left foot and your hand should start somewhere down around your thigh, not necessarily resting on your thigh but just a bit lower than your waist. Toss the sock roll up, trying to keep it in a straight line. If it actually travels in a straight line, you should be able to catch the sock roll without moving your feet. Lefties do the opposite. If you diligently work on your toss, in a short amount of time, it will become a natural part of your service motion.

13. **Keep your tossing arm extended upward.** By keeping your tossing arm extended just a little longer than you think you should, you will prevent the problem of your arm and shoulder dropping too soon as you hit your serve, pulling your body and your racquet off to the side, and reducing your forward swing and power.

14. **Follow through with your serve.** Your service motion is not complete once you hit the ball. Rather, be sure and finish the motion with a complete follow-through. After ball contact, your racquet should continue to travel in a smooth arc. If you do not follow-through completely, you will slow down your service motion. The result will be a slower, softer serve.

15. **Go for your first serve.** You get two serves for a reason - so you can really go for that first serve. Don't hold back on the first serve, trying to just get it in. Relax and go for it!

16. **Get a real second serve.** A "real" second serve is not a puff ball that gets the point started. A real second serve is something that not only goes in most of the time, but also has a little something extra to it. And that something extra is usually spin. Spin can make your serve bounce higher and/or curve off to one side after bouncing. Many players fear a spinny, curving serve more than a straight, flat rocket so it's worth developing a real second serve.

17. **Apply topspin to your serve.** A topspin serve is valuable because it travels quickly and has a high likelihood of landing in. When it bounces, it can leap up and accelerate, often surprising your opponent. To apply topspin to your serve, (1) toss the ball overhead rather than into the court, (2) hit the ball without fully extending your arm, (3) make contact by brushing up across the back of the ball. If the ball is a clock face, you would brush from 7:00 to 1:00 for righties and 5:00 to 11:00 for lefties.

18. **Apply slice to your serve.** A slice serve is great because when it bounces, it stays low and swerves away from the receiver, in the same direction as the spin. (So a right-handed server's slice serve will swerve to the opponent's right.) To apply slice to your serve, (1) use your regular ball toss, slightly into the court, (2) fully extend your arm on contact, (3) brush across the back of the ball from side to side. If the back of the ball is a clock face, brush from 9:00 to 3:00 for righties and from 3:00 to 9:00 for lefties. (4) Follow-through towards your serve target (rather than straight ahead) to maintain the position of your racquet.

19. **Target your serve.** You will control and win more points if you have good placement of your serve. And you can increase the accuracy of your serve by simply having a target. So, before you begin your toss, you should always have a target in mind.

20. **Target your serve up the middle.** A great place to target your serve is up the middle or to the T of the service box. This works especially well if it results in a serve to your opponent's backhand. It is also a good target for setting up your doubles partner to poach.

21. **Target your serve out wide.** Another great target for your serve is out wide, to the far edge of the service box. Hitting this serve will draw your opponent off court, opening up a large area for you to hit into.

22. **Target your serve into your opponent's body.** Targeting your serve into your opponent's body will often jam your opponent, keeping them from using a full, fluid motion to hit their return.

23. **Mix it up.** Do not hit the same serve over and over. Keep your opponent guessing by changing the type of serve you hit and your targets. While a powerful serve can be intimidating, a weak serve can draw a weak return. And a serve that moves around the service box prevents your opponent from ever relaxing on the return.

24. **Rely on your second serve when necessary.** When your first serve is going wrong, rely on your second serve for a game or two, using it in place of your usual first serve. Once you've relaxed by getting your serve in, you'll be ready to go for your first serve again.

25. **Don't think about *not* double faulting.** Just thinking about *not* double faulting means you're thinking about double faulting. Stop! Instead, go through your service ritual, pick a target and hit each of your serves with confidence.

26. **Serve with a plan.** Have a plan for what you will do with the ball after you serve. For example, if you serve up the middle, you can follow with a sharp angle off the court. Or you can do the opposite, serve short and to the outside of the box and follow with a deep shot to the middle. In either case, use your serve to draw your opponent to a certain position and then hit your next shot to the open court.

27. **Serve to set your doubles partner up to poach.** When serving in doubles, be sure to include your partner in your plans. The serve up the middle can set your partner up to poach but will work most effectively if your partner knows that you're targeting your serve there.

28. **Believe in your serve.** Believe that your serve *can* be a weapon. Tennis is truly a mind game. So try to remain confident and positive when serving. Feeling this way, as opposed to feeling insecure and negative, will help you obtain and hit a better serve.

29. **Make it a priority to get your return back.** Do not give your opponent free points by missing your return. A weak return that lands in is better than a powerful return that goes out.

30. **Use a short backswing to block the ball back on your return.** Unless you're consistently receiving a very weak serve, do not use a full takeback on your return. Instead, block the serve back with a short backswing. This is especially effective when you're receiving hard, flat first serves.

31. **Anticipate where the serve is going.** Use the clues that your opponents give you - position on the baseline, type of toss, past experience - to try and anticipate where the serve is going and what type of serve you will receive.

32. **On the return, attack weak second serves.** Your opponent's weak second serve is often the easiest shot you will face in a match. Many players have "bullet" first serves and "marshmallow" second serves. They will avoid double faulting at all costs, resulting in a weak, paceless second serve. So you must attack these and put pressure on your opponent to hit a more aggressive serve.

33. **Hit a deep, hard return.** By hitting a deep, hard return, you keep your opponent pinned back to the baseline.

34. **Hit a short, sharp angle return.** By hitting a short, sharp angle, you draw your opponent off the court, opening the court for your next shot, which should be away from your opponent.

35. **Hit a down-the-line return and hit it early.** The down-the-line return is useful for mixing up your returns and is especially effective in doubles. Even if it is not successful, the early attempt at a down-the-line return pressures your opponent as it puts the thought into his or her mind that you are not afraid to try this return.

36. **Don't forget the lob return.** While the lob return may seem old-fashioned and weak, it can be very effective, especially if hit to the server's backhand. It is an excellent way to mix up your returns and for using in doubles.

37. **Mix up your returns.** If you rely on the same type of return throughout a match, you allow your opponent to relax. Put pressure on him or her by changing up your returns. Even if some of your returns are not as successful as others, by using a variety of returns, you keep pressure on your opponent's serve. This may result in less aggressive serves and possibly more double faults.

STROKES & SHOTS

"The foundation of a winning tennis player is not power and aggression but consistency and control."

- **Greg Moran,** *well-known tennis coach, in his book Tennis Beyond Big Shots*

While even the best tennis tips can't teach you how to hit a tennis stroke, they can teach you how to hit a tennis stroke better. In this chapter, you'll get several tips that will help to improve every stroke or shot you use in a match.

1. **When hitting any shot in tennis, be loose and relaxed.** Don't tighten up when hitting. You can obtain more power and consistency by hitting loose rather than hitting hard.

2. **Choose consistency over power.** The player who wins the point is usually not the one who can hit the hardest. Rather, the point is most often won by the player who consistently gets the ball back and keeps it in.

3. **Make placement a priority.** By moving the ball away from your opponent, placing it where he or she is *not*, you can force your opponent to work harder and hit more shots while out of position.

4. **Use spin to win.** Applying both topspin and slice to your strokes will contribute to the consistency and placement of your strokes. These types of spin will also allow you to hit much harder while still ensuring that your ball stays in.

5. **Prepare by getting in the "ready position."** Too many players start a point by being completely unprepared. Get into the ready position so that you're prepared for whatever comes across the net. This means taking a stance where you face the net, keep your knees soft and slightly bent, and hold the racquet in front of you, with both hands lightly but firmly holding the grip.

6. **Fast feet, slow hands.** Keep your feet moving quickly and get to every shot. Moving to the ball with many small steps is much more effective than lunging at the ball. Keep your upper body still and calm to hit fluidly through your shot.

7. **Take your racquet back early.** Take your racquet back as soon as you determine what kind of shot you're going to hit. This should happen before your opponent's shot crosses the net.

8. **Breathe out as you swing.** Proper breathing will improve your stroke mechanics, give you a more fluid motion, and help calm your mind.

9. **Use a full swing.** A long, full swing is the best way to put spin and power into your shot. This also means including a proper finish to your stroke. Do not stop your stroke early as this will reduce the spin and the pace that you put on the ball.

10. **Keep your feet firmly planted on the ground.** By keeping your feet planted as you hit the ball, rather than jumping up at impact, you will transfer your weight and momentum into the ball, adding more power to your stroke.

11. **Keep your head still and your eyes on the ball.** By keeping your head still and watching the ball hit your racquet, you'll achieve a smoother stroke with a longer follow-through. Avoid the tendency to quickly look up as you hit the ball to see where your shot lands. This can cause you to pull up short on your follow-through.

12.
Don't "guide" the ball. Hit the ball. Don't push it or guide it to where you want it to go. This is especially true when hitting volleys.

13.
Develop "soft hands" to hit touch shots. Some of the hardest shots to return are volleys and drop shots that seem to die after landing. To hit these shots, you need "soft hands," meaning that you know how to take the pace off of the ball. Practice these shots and begin using them in matches as quickly as you can.

14.
Mix up your shots to prevent your opponent from getting comfortable. Even if you can hit hard, line-drive shots that keep your opponent back on the baseline, if this is all you can hit, your opponent may quickly adjust to this and come up with counter measures. Therefore, be sure to have a variety of shots in your arsenal, including touch shots and lobs, to prevent your opponent from getting comfortable with your game.

15.
Hit the perfect lob. Your lob needs to be just right - not too high or deep where it may go

out. But not too low and short where it comes back at you as an overhead smash. Hit your lob just high enough to get over your opponent's head but low enough so that he or she does not have time to run it down.

16. **Add spin to your lob.** By adding spin to your lob, the ball will bounce away from your opponent when it lands, making it that much harder to return.

17. **Add spin to your overhead.** As with the lob, adding spin to your overhead will make it a more difficult shot for your opponent to return and will help keep it in the court.

18. **When you adopt a new stroke, don't look back.** Once you decide to go forward with a new stroke, service motion, or anything else you change in your game, just do it. Don't look back. When you make a change to your game, things might look bad and feel awkward for the first few matches. But just plow on. You will get through it and it will be for the better. At some point, the change you adopt will feel like a natural part of your game and you'll find it hard to even go back to your old ways.

TACTICS & STRATEGY

"Tennis taught me so many lessons in life. One of the things it taught me is that every ball that comes to me, I have to make a decision. I have to accept responsibility for the consequences every time I hit a ball."

- Billie Jean King, *former World No. 1 and winner of 39 Grand Slam titles*

In tennis, tactics are specific actions, or combinations of actions, you take to achieve a single goal. A strategy combines tactics to come up with an overarching game plan for your match. In this chapter, you'll get tips on the basic tactics and strategies that will work in almost every match you play.

1. Play to highlight your strengths and to avoid your weaknesses. Figure out just what your strengths and weaknesses are and then play to set yourself up accordingly. Your strengths are usually the strokes and shots you love to hit over and over. Your weaknesses are the ones that you avoid at all costs. You can find these by thinking about your game, asking your partners and team mates what they think, and talking to your coach during lessons.

2. **Discover and play to your opponent's weaknesses while avoiding their strengths.** It's not enough to play to your own strengths. You must also pay attention throughout your match, probing for, and hopefully playing to, your opponent's weaknesses while avoiding their strengths. In doubles, be sure you're communicating about this with your partner and coming up with tactics and strategies that play to your opponents' weaknesses.

3. **Never hit a second serve.** When you have to hit a second serve, you put yourself under extreme stress and pressure. Your opponent also views your second serve as an opportunity to attack. So up the percentage on your first serves to avoid hitting second serves. You can do this by taking some of the power off your first serve and replacing it with spin for consistency.

4. **Get every return back in play.** Do not give away points by hitting hard, flat returns that end up being out. Instead, block the serve back and keep the ball in play. This is especially true when you're facing a strong first serve. On second serves, the ball is probably coming in slower, giving you a chance to attack.

5. **Hit groundstrokes cross-court.** During a match, the vast majority of your groundstrokes should be hit cross-court, especially in singles. By hitting cross-court, the ball will travel over the middle of the net which is where it's lowest. It will also travel diagonally across the court where the court is longest. This gives you the best chance of having your ball land in.

6. **Hit approach shots straight ahead.** By approaching straight ahead, you give your opponent less time to react since the ball is traveling a shorter distance to get to them. You also put yourself in a better position to cut off whatever angle shot your opponent might hit back.

7. **Take control of the net.** Whether you're playing singles or doubles, controlling the net is the best way to control, and ultimately win, the point. When you're closer into the net, you cut down on your opponent's reaction time. You also create a visually distracting "wall" that will bother your opponent. Just be patient when you're at the net. It may take several shots to finish off the point.

8. **Hit at your opponent's feet.** When you're at the net, the best shot you can hit is at your opponent's feet. Most players do not want to bend down to hit a low ball. Even if your opponent should get to this type of ball, he or she will have to pop the ball up, giving you a great chance at a put-away shot.

9. **When in doubt, lob.** If you're put in a weak position, either deep in the court or off the court completely, don't hesitate to use a lob to buy time to get back into position. This is a great shot for getting back into the point and neutralizing any advantage your opponent may have.

10. **When you hit a good lob, come in.** When you hit a lob that's deep and forces your opponent back, don't waste it. Get into the net to hit a short shot or an angle volley.

11. **Make your opponent work.** Avoid consistently hitting the same ball back to your opponent, over and over. Make your opponent work by mixing things up. Use slice and angles. Change the height of the shot you hit by changing the spin. Change the pace of your shot. Change the speed. Never let your opponent relax.

12. **Hit short shots to the opponent who gets everything back.** A player who gets everything back is often known as a "pusher" or a "moonballer." Playing against a pusher can be frustrating because they don't appear to do anything special. They just get the ball back. If this is not your type of game, you probably won't beat a pusher by trying to adopt it. Instead, hit short balls that draw these players out of their comfort zone on the baseline and into the net.

13. **Use patterns to work your opponent.** Have a plan of at least two shots when you hit the ball, especially when you serve and when you return. Reliable two shot patterns include moving your opponent from side to side and back and forth. Or drawing your opponent off court and then following with a shot into the open court.

14. **Feed your opponent "junk."** Opponents who hit deep, hard shots from the baseline usually love to receive those same shots back. They are not interested in picking up short, dinky shots or in returning loopy moonballs that require creating pace. So give these opponents junky, soft shots and make them work. Take them off the baseline and out of their comfort zone.

15. **Anticipate the shot coming towards you by picking up "clues."** By watching for clues - how your opponent hits the ball, what type of sound is made on contact with the racquet - you can often figure out what type of shot will be coming toward you and get in a good position to respond.

16. **Try to serve and volley.** The serve-and-volley tactic is one of the most basic tactics in tennis, especially in doubles. It works not just because it gets you into the net quickly, but also because it can intimidate and fluster your opponent. If you are not regularly playing serve and volley tennis, you should begin adding it to your tennis tactics right away.

17. **Try the I-Formation in doubles.** In the I-Formation, the server's partner crouches down over the center line of the court and then, when the returner swings, breaks forward to the right or the left, depending upon what he or she has agreed to do with the server. This is an excellent tactic for poaching against a strong returner and, even when unsuccessful, can confuse the opposing team and knock it out of its returning groove.

18. **Don't change the direction of the ball.** When you get into a lob battle, it can be frustrating and you may wish to bring it to a quick end. But the player who attempts to change the direction of the ball is often the player who ends up losing the point. Have patience. Give your opponent a chance to make a change and to make the error.

19. **Play it safe and keep the point alive.** The fewer errors you commit, the more points you're going to win. This means, at times, you need to play it safe and just try to keep the point going. Hopefully, you can cut back on your own errors by giving your opponent the chance to make more of them.

20. **Don't change a winning game.** Don't think about holding onto your win, playing it safe to protect your lead. Rather, continue the playing style that has got you into this position. If being aggressive has done it for you, continue being aggressive. If passively moonballing has gotten you into this position, keep moonballing.

21. **Don't be afraid to change a losing game.**
When your "Plan A" strategy isn't working, don't be afraid to try a completely new "Plan B" strategy. Plan B may be the strategy that ultimately gets the job down and results in a win.

MENTAL STRENGTH & FOCUS

"My greatest point is my persistence. I never give up in a match. However down I am, I fight until the last ball. My list of matches shows that I have turned a great many so-called irretrievable defeats into victories."

- Björn Borg, *former World No. 1 and winner of 11 Grand Slam singles titles*

Tennis is a mental game. If you don't already know that, you need to learn it fast. It's often the mentally stronger player, not necessarily the physically stronger player, who wins the match.

1. **Play winning tennis, not perfect tennis.** The reality of tennis for us "real" players is that matches are won not on the basis of how beautiful our shots are but on how few errors we make. In matches at every

level, the winner is almost always *not* the player with the prettiest shots, but the player who makes the least number of errors. Make it your job to play winning tennis, rather than perfect tennis, by hitting just one more ball in each point than your opponent.

2. **Accept that you will make mistakes.** No player, not even pro tennis players, plays a match without making a mistake. Don't dwell on mistakes. Accept that you will always make them and move on.

3. **Play one point at a time.** Focus completely on what's happening on court in the point you're playing. Do not think about previous errors or the possibility of upcoming flubs. Stay "in the moment" to play your best tennis.

4. **Focus during your match.** Do not chat up your opponent between points or on changeovers. Do not mentally beat yourself up when you make an error. And definitely do not think about what you'll be doing when your match is over. Focus on what's happening on your court during each point of your match.

5. **Narrow your focus.** Avoid the distraction of negative or emotional reactions. Between points, adopt a ritual like keeping your eyes on your strings, on your feet, or on something neutral nearby. Do not think about the score, your opponent, the last point, or even the last shot. When these thoughts intrude, push them aside and go back to your ritual.

6. **Use a mantra for on-court focus.** Repeating a mantra to yourself can help calm your nerves, regulate your breathing, and focus your mind. Your mantra should be short and simple and only needs to make sense to you. Some great tennis mantras to use during a match are:

"Calm and clear."

"Strong and deep."

"I got this."

"Just like practice."

7. **Try to watch the incoming ball hit your strings.** Maintain focus by trying to watch the ball hit the strings of your racquet. While in reality, this is virtually impossible, by trying to do this, you ensure that your mind is not thinking about the score or any errors you've made and you do not turn your head and shoulders away from the ball too early.

8. **Be patient.** You may like points that are quick, with short rallies and someone hitting a definite winner. You may enjoy playing someone who hits hard, line drives right at you. You may prefer a fast game where you have to run every shot down and don't have time to think. However, some opponents will use this against you, wearing you down by just getting the ball back in play and letting you do all of the work and make all of the errors. In this situation, you must be patient. Since all kinds of things may be coming back at you, it might take a few more exchanges to get the right shot that allows you to put the ball away. Don't rush the point. Wait for your opportunity.

9. **Be prepared to work hard.** Even with a weaker opponent, especially with a weaker opponent, you have to do your job. And that means you may have to chase a lot of balls down. It can feel like you're doing all of the work while your opponent is just getting the ball back and not doing much at all. But keep up the work and adopt the strategy of winning the match one point at a time.

10. **Never underestimate your opponent.** Another way to say this is - don't be fooled by appearances. In tennis, looks are often deceiving. That out-of-shape opponent across the net is invariably the master of placement. Or lobbing. Or bullet serving. So don't judge. Always be ready to play a good game of tennis, no matter who shows up on the other side.

11. **Be prepared for inconsistency.** When playing a "weaker opponent," the hardest thing to battle may be their apparent inconsistency. It often seems as if there is very little, if any, logic to their game. You can't come up with your own plan to respond to this type of opponent because you can't figure out what their plan is . So, with these opponents, be on your toes and ready for just about anything to come back across the net.

12. **Don't be fooled by the "lucky shot."** What often happens with some opponents is that they seem to hit a lot of "lucky shots." And before you know it, you've lost the match because of these lucky shots. Do not get into the trap of thinking that your opponent is just playing one lucky shot after another. Some players have very unorthodox strokes or shots that may come off as lucky to you but are repeated over and over throughout a match. Believing that some weird, recurring shot is just "lucky" and will soon come to a stop can lull you into letting up and ultimately losing the match. Instead, pay attention and play every single shot that comes at you.

13. **Learn how to deal with your opponent's bad calls.** When your opponent makes a bad call (or several of them), you have to accept it. No one is perfect with line calls and your opponent is most likely calling the lines as best as he or she can. By getting frustrated, you will not only *not* play your best tennis, you'll play worse. Put your opponent on notice that you're watching these calls with a simple, "are you sure?" and move on. Do not carry negative energy into the next point.

14. **Talk to your doubles partner.** You should always be communicating with your doubles partner. By discussing what is happening during the match, you ensure that you're both on the same page as far as tactics and strategy. You may also point out obvious weaknesses of your opponents that your partner may have missed. Just be sure and keep your communications positive and non-judgmental.

15. **When your strokes are going wrong, go back to the basics.** Do not throw in the towel just because everything seems to be going wrong. Instead, slow down your shots. Don't worry about giving up a few points. Concentrate on getting your strokes back and feeling relaxed.

16. **Put the last point behind you.** Realize that every point, every game, every set is new and different from the previous one. Have faith in your own ability. Push the last point out of your mind and concentrate on winning the next.

17. **Relax.** Calm down. Relax. Enjoy yourself. Tennis is a game after all and getting stressed about it will only lead to you tightening up and playing badly. By relaxing and staying loose, you'll not only play better, you'll have more fun.

TAKE YOUR GAME TO THE NEXT LEVEL

"No matter how good you are, always keep working on your game."

- Michael Jordan, *NBA basketball legend*

There are all kinds of ways to improve your tennis game outside of practicing on court and playing matches. Here are a few of my favorite ways to keep working on my game.

1. **Join a tennis team.** One of the fastest ways to improve your tennis play is to join a tennis team. Not only will you be motivated to hone your skills to win for your team, but you'll be surrounded by other tennis fanatics like yourself, exposing you to unlimited amounts of tennis tips, insights, coaching and help. Tennis teams are available to players of all levels. You can find one by talking to your tennis friends, by asking at your club or neighborhood courts, or even by going on-line. The United States Tennis Association's website is a great resource for finding teams.

2. **Play in a tennis tournament.** Playing in a tournament is a quick way to get better at tennis. Whether you play singles or doubles, a tournament will give you an opportunity to completely immerse yourself in the game for at least a few days. Most tournaments happen over the weekend and guarantee you at least two matches. Many tournaments are now being played using a half-day or short set format for players with little time who are looking for short, quick tournaments.

3. **Become a tennis coach.** Junior teams are always looking for coaching assistance. No matter how short of a time you've been playing the game or how elementary you think your skills are, you can help introduce young players to the game by becoming a recreational or Junior Team Tennis coach. The United States Tennis Association, the United States Professional Tennis Association, the Professional Tennis Registry, and the United States Olympic Committee are working together to train more adults to become tennis coaches for children. You can find more information about coaching by checking out the websites for each of these organizations.

4. **Become a tennis official.** One of the best ways to increase your knowledge about the rules of tennis is to become a United States Tennis Association official. The testing to get started is relatively simple and is available on-line. Yearly training courses will keep you up-to-date on changes to the tennis rules and you can make money by working at tournaments. More information can be found on-line at the USTA's website.

5. **Join a tennis organization.** Simply by joining your national tennis association, you will receive an incredible array of resources and opportunities. The United States Tennis Association, for example, provides members with a monthly written publication in the mail, discounts to tennis retailers and events, as well as several different on-line magazines and on-line resources.

6. **Play tennis for fun.** When every match you play counts for points or ranking or seeding, it's hard to remember that playing tennis for fun can actually help improve your game. When your tennis play doesn't actually "count" for something, you have the opportunity to try out new things in a fun and relaxed atmosphere.

ABOUT THE AUTHOR

Kim Selzman is completely fixated on tennis. She took up the game because her friends told her it was a fun and easy sport and the clothes were very cute. She started as an unathletically-inclined beginner who didn't know her half-volley from her kick serve, but quickly became obsessed with the sport. She now plays on three tennis teams, including one at the Open level. She also works as both a USPTA recreational coach, teaching tennis to children, and as a USTA tennis official, officiating at local tennis tournaments. She is studying to become certified as a Tennis Performance Trainer by the International Tennis Performance Association and is putting together an on-line tennis fitness course for women.

Kim chronicles all of her on-court adventures over at *TennisFixation.com* and hosts a weekly iTunes podcast called *Tennis Quick Tips*. She is the author of the free ebook, *10 "Quick Fixes" to Improve Your*

Serve: No Lessons Required which can be found at *TennisFixation.com*.

Printed in Great Britain
by Amazon